BAD GU[...]

FEATURED IN THE NETFLIX SERIES

BRIDGERTON

ORIGINALLY RECORDED BY
BILLIE EILISH

WORDS AND MUSIC BY
BILLIE EILISH O'CONNELL AND FINNEAS O'CONNELL

AS ARRANGED BY KATHY MCMILLEN FOR

VITAMIN STRING QUARTET

ISBN 978-1-7051-3466-5

VSQ
Vitamin String Quartet

DISTRIBUTED BY
HAL•LEONARD®

Visit Hal Leonard Online at
www.halleonard.com

Contact us:
Hal Leonard
7777 West Bluemound Road
Milwaukee, WI 53213
Email: info@halleonard.com

In Europe, contact:
Hal Leonard Europe Limited
42 Wigmore Street
Marylebone, London, W1U 2RN
Email: info@halleonardeurope.com

In Australia, contact:
Hal Leonard Australia Pty. Ltd.
4 Lentara Court
Cheltenham, Victoria, 3192 Australia
Email: info@halleonard.com.au

BAD GUY

Words and Music by
Billie Eilish O'Connell and Finneas O'Connell
As arranged by Kathy McMillen
for Vitamin String Quartet

BAD GUY

FEATURED IN THE NETFLIX SERIES

BRIDGERTON

ORIGINALLY RECORDED BY
BILLIE EILISH

WORDS AND MUSIC BY
BILLIE EILISH O'CONNELL AND FINNEAS O'CONNELL

AS ARRANGED BY KATHY MCMILLEN FOR

VITAMIN STRING QUARTET

ISBN 978-1-7051-3466-5

Vitamin String Quartet

DISTRIBUTED BY

Visit Hal Leonard Online at
www.halleonard.com

Contact us:
Hal Leonard
7777 West Bluemound Road
Milwaukee, WI 53213
Email: info@halleonard.com

In Europe, contact:
Hal Leonard Europe Limited
42 Wigmore Street
Marylebone, London, W1U 2RN
Email: info@halleonardeurope.com

In Australia, contact:
Hal Leonard Australia Pty. Ltd.
4 Lentara Court
Cheltenham, Victoria, 3192 Australia
Email: info@halleonard.com.au

BAD GUY

**Words and Music by
Billie Eilish O'Connell and Finneas O'Connell
As arranged by Kathy McMillen
for Vitamin String Quartet**

BAD GUY

FEATURED IN THE NETFLIX SERIES

BRIDGERTON

ORIGINALLY RECORDED BY
BILLIE EILISH

WORDS AND MUSIC BY
BILLIE EILISH O'CONNELL AND FINNEAS O'CONNELL

AS ARRANGED BY KATHY MCMILLEN FOR

VITAMIN STRING QUARTET

ISBN 978-1-7051-3466-5

VSQ
Vitamin String Quartet

DISTRIBUTED BY
Hal•Leonard

Visit Hal Leonard Online at
www.halleonard.com

Contact us:
Hal Leonard
7777 West Bluemound Road
Milwaukee, WI 53213
Email: info@halleonard.com

In Europe, contact:
Hal Leonard Europe Limited
42 Wigmore Street
Marylebone, London, W1U 2RN
Email: info@halleonardeurope.com

In Australia, contact:
Hal Leonard Australia Pty. Ltd.
4 Lentara Court
Cheltenham, Victoria, 3192 Australia
Email: info@halleonard.com.au

BAD GUY

Words and Music by
Billie Eilish O'Connell and Finneas O'Connell
As arranged by Kathy McMillen
for Vitamin String Quartet

BAD GUY

FEATURED IN THE NETFLIX SERIES

BRIDGERTON

ORIGINALLY RECORDED BY
BILLIE EILISH

WORDS AND MUSIC BY
BILLIE EILISH O'CONNELL AND FINNEAS O'CONNELL

AS ARRANGED BY KATHY MCMILLEN FOR

VITAMIN STRING QUARTET

ISBN 978-1-7051-3466-5

Vitamin String Quartet

DISTRIBUTED BY

Visit Hal Leonard Online at
www.halleonard.com

Contact us:
Hal Leonard
7777 West Bluemound Road
Milwaukee, WI 53213
Email: info@halleonard.com

In Europe, contact:
Hal Leonard Europe Limited
42 Wigmore Street
Marylebone, London, W1U 2RN
Email: info@halleonardeurope.com

In Australia, contact:
Hal Leonard Australia Pty. Ltd.
4 Lentara Court
Cheltenham, Victoria, 3192 Australia
Email: info@halleonard.com.au

VIOLA

BAD GUY

Words and Music by
Billie Eilish O'Connell and Finneas O'Connell
As arranged by Kathy McMillen
for Vitamin String Quartet

BAD GUY

FEATURED IN THE NETFLIX SERIES

BRIDGERTON

ORIGINALLY RECORDED BY
BILLIE EILISH

WORDS AND MUSIC BY
BILLIE EILISH O'CONNELL AND FINNEAS O'CONNELL

AS ARRANGED BY KATHY MCMILLEN FOR
VITAMIN STRING QUARTET

ISBN 978-1-7051-3466-5

Vitamin String Quartet

DISTRIBUTED BY

Visit Hal Leonard Online at
www.halleonard.com

Contact us:
Hal Leonard
7777 West Bluemound Road
Milwaukee, WI 53213
Email: info@halleonard.com

In Europe, contact:
Hal Leonard Europe Limited
42 Wigmore Street
Marylebone, London, W1U 2RN
Email: info@halleonardeurope.com

In Australia, contact:
Hal Leonard Australia Pty. Ltd.
4 Lentara Court
Cheltenham, Victoria, 3192 Australia
Email: info@halleonard.com.au

BAD GUY

CELLO

Words and Music by
Billie Eilish O'Connell and Finneas O'Connell
As arranged by Kathy McMillen
for Vitamin String Quartet

Pop ♩=135

not too heavily accented
on beat 4